meals in minutes

simple suppers

RECIPES
Melanie Barnard

PHOTOGRAPHS
Bill Bettencourt

weldonowen

contents

30 MINUTES START TO FINISH

about this book

People are often far too busy to spend time in the kitchen at the end of the day. Meals in Minutes *Simple Suppers* puts to test the notion that a healthy, home-cooked meal is a difficult undertaking. In the pages that follow, you will find recipes designed to teach you that the simplest of ingredients, when prepared correctly, can create quick and satisfying meals for any day of the week.

Classics such as crispy Pork Schnitzel, flavorful Chicken Saltimbocca, and tender Steak au Poivre can be on the table in under 30 minutes. Other recipes include hearty Balsamic Beef Stew and crunchy Oven-Fried Chicken, which require only 15 minutes hands-on time. Recipes such as traditional Roast Pork Loin with Pan Sauce make enough to eat throughout the week and can be turned into other recipes such as Pork Lo Mein. Round these main dishes out with a mixed green salad and steamed rice, and you have a healthy, stress-free meal.

30 minutes
start to finish

chicken in orange-riesling sauce

Orange, 1 large

Skinless, boneless chicken breast halves, 4, 1½ lb (750 g) total weight

Salt and freshly ground pepper

Unsalted butter, 3 tablespoons

Shallot, 1, minced

Riesling or other fruity white wine, ½ cup (4 fl oz/125 ml)

Fresh marjoram, 1 tablespoon finely chopped

SERVES 4

1 **Prepare the orange and chicken**
Finely grate 2 teaspoons zest and squeeze ¼ cup (2 fl oz/60 ml) juice from the orange. Set the zest and juice aside. Place 1 chicken breast half between 2 sheets of waxed paper. Using a meat pounder or the flat bottom of a heavy pan, lightly pound the chicken until it is about ½ inch (12 mm) thick. Repeat with the remaining chicken breast halves. Season generously with salt and pepper.

2 **Cook the chicken**
In a large frying pan over medium-high heat, melt 2 tablespoons of the butter. Working in batches, if needed, to avoid crowding, add the chicken and cook, turning once, until golden on both sides and opaque throughout, 6–8 minutes total. Transfer the chicken to a plate.

3 **Make the sauce**
Melt the remaining 1 tablespoon butter in the pan over medium heat. Add the shallot and sauté until lightly browned, about 1 minute. Add the wine, marjoram, and reserved orange juice and zest. Cook, stirring to scrape up the browned bits on the pan bottom, until the sauce is bubbly and slightly reduced, about 3 minutes. Return the chicken and any juices from the plate to the pan and heat through, about 1 minute. Season to taste with salt and pepper. Transfer to a platter, spoon the sauce over the chicken, and serve.

cook's tip

Always grate the zest before juicing any citrus fruit. Grate only the colored part of the peel, avoiding the bitter white pith beneath it. A handheld rasp grater is the best tool for finely grated zest.

cook's tip

Lemongrass, a popular Asian
ingredient, is available in many
markets. Use only the bulb
portion of the stalk, and remove
the tough outer layers before
chopping. If you can't find
lemongrass, you can substitute
1 tablespoon lemon juice and
2 teaspoons grated lemon zest.
Add them along with the garlic
and ginger in Step 1.

ginger chicken & green onions

1 Stir-fry the chicken

Season the chicken generously with salt and pepper. In a wok or large frying pan over high heat, warm the oil. Add the chicken and stir-fry until golden and nearly cooked through, 3–4 minutes. Add the garlic, ginger, lemongrass, and half of the green onions and stir-fry just until fragrant, about 30 seconds.

2 Finish the dish

Add the broth and fish sauce to the pan, reduce the heat to medium, and simmer until the chicken is opaque throughout and the sauce is slightly reduced, 2–3 minutes longer. Sprinkle with the remaining green onions and the mint, and serve with the rice.

Skinless, boneless chicken breast halves, 1½ lb (750 g) total weight, cut into thin strips

Salt and freshly ground pepper

Peanut or canola oil, 3 tablespoons

Garlic, 4 cloves, minced

Ginger, 3 tablespoons minced

Lemongrass, 2 tablespoons finely chopped

Green (spring) onions, 4, thinly sliced

Chicken broth, ⅔ cup (5 fl oz/150 ml)

Asian fish sauce, 2 tablespoons

Fresh mint, 2 tablespoons chopped

Steamed rice, for serving

SERVES 4

pork schnitzel with arugula

Lemons, 2

Coarse fresh bread crumbs, 1 ½ cups (3 oz/90 g)

Flour, ⅓ cup (1 ½ oz/45 g)

Salt and freshly ground pepper

Egg, 1

Boneless pork cutlets, 4, 1 ½ lb (750 g) total weight

Olive oil, 4 tablespoons (2 fl oz/60 ml)

Shallot, 1, minced

Arugula (rocket) or frisée, 6 oz (185 g), tough stems removed

SERVES 4

1 Bread the pork

Finely grate 2 teaspoons zest and squeeze 2 tablespoons juice from 1 lemon. Cut the second lemon into 8 wedges. Spread the bread crumbs on a plate. On another plate, stir together the flour, lemon zest, ½ teaspoon salt, and ¼ teaspoon pepper. In a shallow bowl, whisk the egg with 1 ½ tablespoons water. Place 1 pork cutlet between 2 sheets of waxed paper. Using a meat pounder or the flat bottom of a heavy pan, lightly pound the pork until it is about ½ inch (12 mm) thick. Repeat with the remaining cutlets. Dip both sides of each cutlet in the flour, then in the egg, and finally in the crumbs, coating evenly and patting them firmly so they adhere. (The pork cutlets can be prepared, covered, and refrigerated up to 3 hours in advance.)

2 Cook the pork

In a large frying pan over medium-high heat, warm 2 tablespoons of the oil. Add the cutlets and cook, turning once, until golden brown on both sides and barely pink in the center, 4–6 minutes total. Transfer to a plate.

3 Make the salad

Add the remaining 2 tablespoons oil to the pan over medium heat. Add the shallots and sauté until softened, about 1 minute. Stir in the lemon juice, scraping up the browned bits on the pan bottom. Remove from the heat, add the arugula, and toss briefly to coat with the dressing. Divide the cutlets among dinner plates and top with the arugula mixture. Garnish with the lemon wedges and serve.

beef & asparagus stir-fry

1 Cook the beef and vegetables

Lightly season the beef with salt and pepper. In a small
bowl, stir together the hoisin sauce, sherry, chile oil, and ½ cup
(4 fl oz/125 ml) water. In a wok or large frying pan over high
heat, warm the peanut oil. Working in batches if needed to avoid
crowding, add the beef and cook, turning once or twice, until
lightly seared, 2–3 minutes. Using a slotted spoon, transfer
to a plate. Add the onion and asparagus to the pan and cook
until tender-crisp, 2–3 minutes. Add the garlic and red pepper
flakes and stir-fry for 15 seconds.

2 Finish the dish

Return the meat and any juices from the plate to the
pan, add the hoisin mixture, and mix well. Simmer briefly
until heated through. Divide the rice among shallow bowls,
top with beef and asparagus, and serve.

Sirloin steak, 1 ½ lb (750 g),
cut into thin strips

**Salt and freshly ground
pepper**

Hoisin sauce, ¼ cup
(2 fl oz/60 ml)

Dry sherry, 2 tablespoons

Chile oil, 1 teaspoon

Peanut oil, ¼ cup
(2 fl oz/ 60 ml)

Yellow onion, 1, thinly sliced

Slender asparagus, ¾ lb
(375 g), trimmed and cut
on the diagonal into 1-inch
(2.5-cm) pieces

Garlic, 3 cloves, minced

Red pepper flakes,
¼ teaspoon

Steamed rice, for serving

SERVES 4

penne with basil & pine nuts

Salt and freshly ground pepper

Penne, 1 lb (500 g)

Pine nuts, ⅓ cup (2 oz/60 g)

Olive oil, 6 tablespoons (3 fl oz/90 ml)

Fine bread crumbs, 1 cup (2 oz/60 g)

Garlic, 3 cloves, minced

Dry white wine, 1 cup (8 fl oz/250 ml)

Red pepper flakes, ¼ teaspoon

Parmesan cheese, ¼ lb (125 g), freshly grated

Fresh basil leaves, ⅔ cup (1 oz/30 g) slivered

SERVES 4

1 Cook the pasta

Bring a large pot of water to a boil. Add 2 tablespoons salt and the pasta. Cook, stirring occasionally to prevent sticking, until the pasta is al dente, according to package directions. Drain and return to the pot.

2 Prepare the sauce

Meanwhile, in a large sauté pan over medium-high heat, toast pine nuts, stirring often, until fragrant and golden, about 2 minutes. Transfer to a small bowl. Add 1 tablespoon of the oil to the pan, add the bread crumbs, and toss until toasted and golden, 1–2 minutes. Add to the bowl with the pine nuts and stir to mix. Reduce the heat to medium and add 1 tablespoon of the oil to the pan. Add the garlic and sauté until fragrant, about 30 seconds. Stir in the wine and red pepper flakes, bring to a boil, and simmer until slightly reduced, about 2 minutes.

3 Finish the dish

Add the hot pasta along with the remaining 4 tablespoons (2 fl oz/60 ml) oil to the wine sauce in the pan and toss to coat the pasta. Add the bread crumb mixture, the cheese, and the basil and toss to combine. Season with salt and pepper. Divide among shallow bowls and serve.

cook's tip

To make fresh bread crumbs, use day-old bread, ideally from a baguette or country loaf. Alternatively, dry fresh slices in a 300°F (150°C) oven for about 10 minutes. Tear the bread into large pieces and process in a food processor to make crumbs.

cook's tip

You can substitute 4 skinless,
boneless chicken breast halves
for the veal scallops. Place each
breast half between 2 sheets
of waxed paper and lightly pound
with a meat pounder or the flat
bottom of a heavy pan until it
is ¼ inch (6 mm) thick. Serve
with sautéed green beans.

veal
piccata

1 Cook the veal

Season the veal with salt and pepper. In a large frying pan over medium-high heat melt 1½ tablespoons of the butter. Add half of the veal and cook, turning once, until browned, about 2 minutes total. Transfer to a plate. Repeat with 1½ tablespoons of butter and the remaining veal. Be careful not to overcook.

2 Make the sauce

Add the remaining 1 tablespoon butter to the pan and melt over medium-high heat. Add the garlic and sauté until fragrant, about 30 seconds. Add the broth and wine and cook, stirring to scrape up the browned bits on the pan bottom, until the sauce is reduced by about one-fourth, 2–3 minutes. Stir in the capers and simmer for 1 minute. Season to taste with salt and pepper and add the parsley. Return the veal and any juices to the pan and cook until heated through, about 2 minutes. Divide the veal among dinner plates, spoon the sauce over the veal, and serve.

Veal scallops, 8, about 1½ lb (750 g) total weight, pounded to about ¼ inch (6 mm) thickness

Salt and freshly ground pepper

Unsalted butter, 4 tablespoons (2 oz/60 g)

Garlic, 2 large cloves, minced

Chicken broth, ½ cup (4 fl oz/125 ml)

Dry white wine, ½ cup (4 fl oz/125 ml)

Capers, 2 tablespoons

Fresh flat-leaf (Italian) parsley or chervil, 2 tablespoons chopped

SERVES 4

chile-rubbed pork with corn salsa

Pork tenderloins,
2, about 1½ lb (750 g)
total weight

Olive oil, 2 tablespoons

**Salt and freshly ground
pepper**

Ancho chile powder,
2 teaspoons

**Fresh or thawed frozen
corn kernels,** 1 cup
(6 oz/185 g)

Ground cumin, ¾ teaspoon

Yellow onion, 1 small,
chopped

Tomato, 1 large, seeded
and chopped

Lime juice, from 1 lime

**Fresh cilantro (fresh
coriander),** 3 tablespoons
chopped

SERVES 4–6

1 Roast the pork
Preheat the oven to 425°F (230°C). Rub the pork
with 1 tablespoon of the oil, then season generously with salt,
pepper, and the chile powder. In a large frying pan over
medium-high heat, warm the remaining 1 tablespoon oil.
Add the pork and brown on all sides, about 5 minutes
total. Transfer the tenderloins to a shallow roasting pan just
large enough to hold them. Reserve the frying pan and
drippings. Roast the pork until an instant-read thermometer
inserted into the center registers 145°–150°F (63°–65°C)
and the meat is barely pink in the center, 15–20 minutes.
Transfer the pork to a carving board, tent with aluminum
foil, and let stand for 10 minutes.

2 Make the salsa
While the pork rests, add the corn and cumin to the
drippings in the frying pan and place over medium-high heat.
Cook, stirring, until the corn is lightly browned, 3–4 minutes.
Remove from the heat and stir in the onion, tomato, lime juice,
and cilantro. Season to taste with salt and pepper. Cut the
pork into thin slices and serve with the warm salsa.

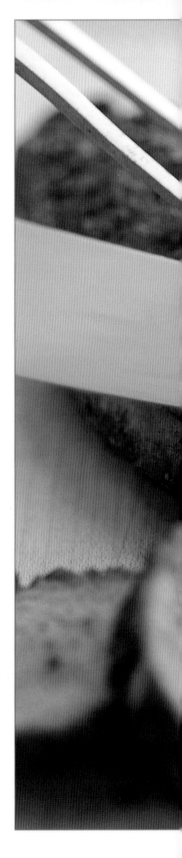

cook's tip

Serve roasted sweet potatoes
on the side for a complete meal.
Peel and halve 4 sweet potatoes
and cut into wedges. Toss with
1 tablespoon vegetable oil, salt,
and pepper, and arrange in
a single layer on a baking sheet.
Roast the sweet potato wedges
alongside the pork, turning them
once, until crispy and browned,
about 20 minutes.

sesame chicken with sugar snap peas

1 Prepare the chicken

Season the chicken with salt and pepper, then sprinkle with the sesame seeds, coating evenly and patting firmly so they adhere to the meat.

2 Cook the chicken and vegetables

In a wok or large frying pan over high heat, warm the peanut oil. Add the chicken and cook, stirring often, until golden and nearly cooked through, 3–4 minutes. Using a slotted spoon, transfer the chicken to a plate. Add the bell pepper, sugar snap peas, and garlic and stir-fry just until the vegetables are barely tender-crisp, 1–2 minutes.

3 Finish the dish

Return the chicken to the pan and add the broth, soy sauce, vinegar, and sesame oil. Reduce the heat to medium and simmer until the chicken is opaque throughout and the sauce is slightly reduced, about 2 minutes. Divide the chicken and vegetables among shallow bowls, sprinkle with the cilantro, and serve.

Skinless, boneless chicken breast halves, 1 1/2 lb (750 g) total weight, cut into thin strips

Salt and freshly ground pepper

Sesame seeds, 3 tablespoons

Peanut oil, 3 tablespoons

Red bell pepper (capsicum), 1, seeded and cut into thin strips

Sugar snap peas, 1/2 lb (250 g)

Garlic, 3 cloves, minced

Chicken broth, 2/3 cup (5 fl oz/150 ml)

Soy sauce, 3 tablespoons

Rice vinegar, 2 tablespoons

Asian sesame oil, 1 tablespoon

Fresh cilantro (fresh coriander), 1/4 cup (1/3 oz/ 10 g) chopped

SERVES 4

25

pork with orange-bourbon sauce

Boneless pork cutlets,
4, 1½ lb (750 g)
total weight

**Salt and freshly ground
pepper**

Fresh thyme, 1 tablespoon
chopped

Unsalted butter,
3 tablespoons

Red onion, 1 small,
thinly sliced

Fresh orange juice, ⅓ cup
(3 fl oz/80 ml)

Bourbon, or Madeira,
2 tablespoons

SERVES 4

1 Cook the pork
Season the pork generously with salt and pepper.
Sprinkle with the thyme, patting firmly so it adheres to the meat.
In a large frying pan over medium-high heat, melt 2 tablespoons
of the butter. Add the pork and cook, turning once, until
browned on both sides and barely pink in the center, about
8 minutes total. Transfer to a plate.

2 Make the sauce
Add the onion to the pan and sauté over medium heat
until softened, about 4 minutes. Add the orange juice and
bourbon to the pan and cook, stirring to scrape up the browned
bits on the pan bottom, about 1 minute. Return the meat
and any juices from the plate to the pan, cover, and cook until
heated through, about 1 minute. Transfer to a carving board
and let rest briefly, about 2 minutes. Arrange the pork and onion
mixture on a platter or divide among dinner plates, spoon
the sauce over the top, and serve.

cook's tip

To test pork for doneness,
insert an instant-read
thermometer into the
thickest part of the meat.
The thermometer should

register at least 145°–150°F
(63°–65°C) for medium.
Note that the temperature
will rise 5°–10°F (3°–6°C)
while resting.

cook's tip

To make this a complete meal,
serve the turkey meatballs and
homemade cranberry sauce
with creamy mashed potatoes
and a green vegetable such
as green beans or broccoli.

herbed turkey meatballs

1 Make the meatballs

Preheat the oven to 425°F (220°C) and lightly oil a rimmed baking sheet. In a large frying pan over medium-high heat, melt the butter. Add the onion and celery and sauté until softened, 4–5 minutes. Spoon into a bowl and let cool, and set the frying pan aside. Add the turkey, bread crumbs, egg, oregano, and ½ teaspoon each salt and pepper to the cooled onion mixture, and mix gently but thoroughly with your hands. Shape the mixture into 12 meatballs and arrange on the prepared baking sheet.

2 Cook the meatballs and make the sauce

Bake the meatballs until opaque throughout, about 10 minutes. Meanwhile, combine the orange juice, cranberries, and sugar in the frying pan and place over medium-high heat. Cook, stirring often, until the juice comes to a boil and the cranberries begin to pop, 2–3 minutes. Divide the meatballs among dinner plates, spoon the sauce over them, and serve.

Unsalted butter,
1 tablespoon

Yellow onion, ½, finely chopped

Celery, 1 small rib, finely chopped

Ground (minced) turkey,
1 lb (500 g)

Fine fresh bread crumbs,
1 cup (2 oz/60 g)

Egg, 1

Fresh oregano,
2 tablespoons chopped

Salt and freshly ground pepper

Orange juice, ⅔ cup
(5 fl oz/150 ml)

Fresh or frozen cranberries, 1 cup
(4 oz/125 g)

Sugar, ¼ cup (2 oz/60 g)

SERVES 4

steak
au poivre

Peppercorns, 1 tablespoon

Coarse sea salt,
1 tablespoon

**Rib-eye or New York strip
steaks,** 4, each about 6 oz
(185 g) and 1 inch (2.5 cm)
thick

Unsalted butter,
3 tablespoons

Canola oil, 1 tablespoon

Shallots, 2, thinly sliced

Cognac or brandy, ⅓ cup
(3 fl oz/80 ml)

Heavy (double) cream,
⅓ cup (3 fl oz/80 ml)

Fresh tarragon, 1 teaspoon
chopped (optional)

**Salt and freshly ground
pepper**

SERVES 4

1 **Prepare the steaks**
Place the peppercorns in a small, heavy-duty resealable plastic bag. Coarsely crush them with a rolling pin. In a small dish, stir together the crushed peppercorns and the coarse salt. Pat the mixture firmly and evenly on both sides of the steaks.

2 **Cook the steaks**
In a large frying pan (or 2 medium pans) over medium-high heat, melt 2 tablespoons of the butter with the oil. Add the steaks and cook, turning once, for 6–8 minutes total for medium-rare, or until done to your liking. Transfer the steaks to a platter and tent with aluminum foil.

3 **Make the sauce**
Add the remaining 1 tablespoon butter to the pan and place over medium heat. Add the shallots and sauté until softened, about 1 minute. Stir in the Cognac, cream, and tarragon and bring just to a boil, stirring up the browned bits on the pan bottom. Lower the heat and simmer until slightly thickened, about 1 minute. Season to taste with salt and pepper. Divide the steaks among dinner plates, spoon the sauce and shallots over them, and serve.

cook's tip

For a lighter dish, omit the
Cognac, cream, and tarragon.
Add ½ lb (250 g) thinly sliced
cremini mushrooms to the pan
with the shallots and sauté
until tender, about 5 minutes.
Season to taste with salt
and pepper and serve over
the steak.

cook's tip

If you do not have a meat pounder or a suitable heavy pan, you can use a rolling pin to pound the chicken with equally good results.

chicken saltimbocca

1 Prepare the chicken

Preheat the broiler (grill). Using a sharp knife, cut each chicken breast in half lengthwise to make 8 pieces total. Place 1 piece between 2 sheets of waxed paper. Using a meat pounder or the flat bottom of a heavy pan, lightly pound the chicken until it is about ¼ inch (6 mm) thick. Repeat with the remaining pieces. Season the chicken generously with salt and pepper, then sprinkle with the sage, patting firmly so it adheres to the meat.

2 Cook the chicken

In a large frying pan (or 2 medium pans) over medium-high heat, melt 3 tablespoons of the butter. Add the chicken and cook until golden on the underside, 2–3 minutes. Turn the chicken and cook until just opaque throughout, about 3 minutes more. Top each piece with 1 cheese slice and 1 prosciutto slice. Transfer the chicken to a baking sheet and place under the broiler to crisp the prosciutto and melt the cheese, about 1 minute.

3 Make the sauce

While the chicken is in the oven, add the remaining 1 tablespoon butter to the pan(s). Add the shallot and sauté until softened, about 1 minute. Add the Marsala and cook, stirring to scrape up the browned bits on the pan bottom, until the sauce is slightly reduced, 1–2 minutes. Squeeze in about 1 teaspoon lemon juice and stir. Divide the chicken among dinner plates, spoon the sauce and shallots over the chicken, and serve immediately.

Skinless, boneless chicken breasts halves, 4, 1½ lb (750 g) total weight

Salt and freshly ground pepper

Fresh sage, 2 tablespoons chopped

Unsalted butter, 4 tablespoons (2 oz/60 g)

Prosciutto or boiled ham, 4 large thin slices, halved about 2 oz (60 g) total weight

Fontina cheese, 8 thin slices about 3 oz (90 g) total weight

Shallots, 2, minced

Marsala, or chicken broth, ½ cup (4 fl oz/125 ml)

Lemon, ½

SERVES 4–6

braised pork chops with cherry sauce

Bone-in, center-cut pork loin chops, 4, each ¾ inch (2 cm) thick

Salt and freshly ground pepper

Fresh rosemary, 1 tablespoon minced

Unsalted butter, 3 tablespoons

Leeks, 2, including pale green parts, halved, rinsed, and thinly sliced

Chicken broth, 1 cup (8 fl oz/250 ml)

Port wine, ¼ cup (2 fl oz/60 ml)

Balsamic vinegar, 2 tablespoons

Dried cherries, ½ cup (2 oz/60 g)

SERVES 4

1 Brown the pork chops
Season the pork chops with salt, pepper, and the rosemary, patting them firmly to adhere to the meat. In a large frying pan over medium-high heat, melt 2 tablespoons of the butter. Add the pork chops and cook, turning once, until golden on both sides, about 6 minutes total. Transfer the pork to a plate.

2 Make the sauce
Melt the remaining 1 tablespoon butter in the pan over medium heat. Add the leeks and sauté until softened and beginning to brown, 3–4 minutes. Stir in the broth and cook, stirring to scrape up the browned bits on the pan bottom, for 1 minute. Stir in the wine, vinegar, and the cherries.

3 Finish the dish
Return the pork chops and any juices from the plate to the pan and spoon the liquid over them. Cover, reduce the heat to medium-low, and simmer until the pork is tender and barely pink in the center, about 15 minutes. Divide the chops among dinner plates, spoon the sauce over them, and serve.

cook's tip

Always let meat rest before
carving, allowing the juices
that accumulate while cooking
to redistribute themselves
throughout the piece of meat.
While resting, the temperature
of the meat can rise 5°–10°F
(3°–6°C).

steak
piperade

1 Brown the steak

Season the steak generously with salt and pepper. In a large frying pan over high heat, warm 1 tablespoon each of the butter and oil. Add the steak and cook, turning once, for 4–6 minutes total for medium-rare, or until done to your liking. Transfer the meat to a carving board and tent with aluminum foil.

2 Make the sauce

Warm the remaining 1 tablespoon each butter and oil in the pan over medium heat. Add the onion, peppers, garlic, and thyme and sauté until the onion is barely softened, 3–4 minutes. Add the wine, bring to a boil, stirring to scrape up the browned bits on the pan bottom, and boil for about 30 seconds. Stir in the tomatoes and their juice and simmer until the liquid is slightly reduced, about 5 minutes. Season to taste with salt and pepper.

3 Slice the meat

Slice the meat thinly across the grain on the diagonal. Arrange the slices on dinner plates or on a serving platter, spoon the sauce over the slices, and serve.

Skirt or flank steak, 1 ½ lb (750 g)

Salt and freshly ground pepper

Unsalted butter, 2 tablespoons

Olive oil, 2 tablespoons

Red onion, 1, chopped

Red or yellow bell peppers (capsicums), 3, seeded and thinly sliced crosswise

Garlic, 3 cloves, minced

Fresh thyme, 1 tablespoon chopped

Dry white wine, ½ cup (4 fl oz/125 ml)

Diced tomatoes, 1 can (14½ oz/455 g)

SERVES 4

tequila-marinated skirt steak

Limes, 3

Canola oil, ¼ cup
(2 fl oz/ 60 ml)

Tequila, 3 tablespoons

Sugar, 1 teaspoon

Salt

Skirt steak, 1½ lb
(750 g), cut into 8-inch
(20-cm) lengths

Unsalted butter, ½ cup
(4 oz/125 g), at room
temperature

Ancho chile powder,
2 teaspoons

SERVES 4

1 **Marinate the steak**
Finely grate the zest from the limes and squeeze
3 tablespoons juice. In a shallow dish large enough to hold
the meat in a single layer, stir together the lime juice, oil,
tequila, sugar, and ½ teaspoon salt. Add the meat and turn
to coat. Cover and let marinate at room temperature for
about 15 minutes.

2 **Make the ancho-lime butter**
Prepare a gas or charcoal grill for direct-heat grilling
over high heat and oil the grill rack, or preheat a stovetop grill
pan over high heat. Meanwhile, in a small bowl, combine the
butter, lime zest, and chile powder. Set aside.

3 **Cook the steak**
Remove the meat from the marinade, discarding the
marinade. Place on the grill rack or grill pan and cook, turning
once, for 4–6 minutes for medium-rare, or until done to your
liking. Let stand for 2 minutes on a carving board, then thinly
slice across the grain. Divide the steak among dinner plates
and spoon any meat juices over the slices. Add a spoonful
of the ancho-lime butter atop the steak slices and serve.
Wrap the remainder of the butter in plastic wrap and place
in the freezer for another use (see Cook's Tip).

cook's tip

Make extra butter to serve with grilled corn, roasted vegetables, or roasted or grilled pork. The butter can be shaped into a log, wrapped in plastic wrap, and frozen for up to 1 month. Cut slices from the log as needed.

15 minutes
hands-on time

braised chicken, tomatoes & bacon

Thick-cut bacon, 4 slices, chopped

Bone-in, skin on chicken thighs, 6, 2 lb (1 kg) total weight

Salt and freshly ground pepper

Yellow onion, 1, chopped

Garlic, 2 large cloves, minced

Dry white wine, ¼ cup (2 fl oz/60 ml)

Fresh oregano, 1 tablespoon chopped

Red pepper flakes, ¼ teaspoon

Diced tomatoes, 1 can (14½ oz/455 g), with juice

SERVES 4–6

1 Cook the bacon
In a large frying pan over medium heat, cook the bacon, turning often, until crisp, 4–5 minutes. Using a slotted spoon, transfer the bacon to a small plate. Drain off all but 2 tablespoons drippings from the pan.

2 Brown the chicken
Season the chicken with salt and pepper. Return the pan to medium-high heat, add the chicken, and cook, turning once or twice, until golden brown on both sides, about 8 minutes total. Transfer the chicken to a plate. Add the onion and garlic to the pan and sauté until softened, about 4 minutes.

3 Braise the chicken
Pour in the wine and stir to scrape up the browned bits on the pan bottom. Stir in the oregano, red pepper flakes, and tomatoes and their juice. Return the chicken and any juices from the plate to the pan, cover, reduce the heat to medium-low, and braise until the chicken is cooked through, 25–30 minutes. Uncover, raise the heat to medium-high, bring to a simmer, and stir in the bacon. Transfer the chicken to dinner plates, top with the sauce, and serve.

cook's tip

To complete the menu, serve with egg noodles or mashed potatoes and a green salad. This dish can be prepared

up to 1 day ahead to allow time for the flavors to blend. Reheat, covered, on the stovetop over medium-low heat, until warmed throughout.

braised chicken with mushrooms

1 Brown the chicken

Season the chicken generously with salt and pepper. In a large frying pan over medium-high heat, melt 2 tablespoons of the butter. Add the chicken and cook, turning once or twice, until golden brown on both sides, about 8 minutes total. Transfer the chicken to a plate.

2 Cook the vegetables

Melt the remaining 1 tablespoon butter in the pan over medium heat. Add the onion and sauté until barely softened, about 3 minutes. Add the mushrooms and sauté until their juices are released, about 5 minutes. Stir in the Madeira and Worcestershire sauce.

3 Braise the chicken

Return the chicken and any juices from the plate to the pan, and spoon the mushrooms over the chicken. Cover, reduce the heat to medium-low, and braise the chicken until opaque throughout, 20–25 minutes. Stir in the tarragon and season to taste with salt and pepper. Divide the chicken among dinner plates, spoon the mushrooms over the chicken, and serve.

Bone-in, skin on chicken breast halves, 4, 1 ½ lb (750 g) total weight

Salt and freshly ground pepper

Unsalted butter, 3 tablespoons

Yellow onion, 1 small, chopped

Wild and/or cultivated mushrooms, 1 lb (500 g), sliced

Madeira or dry sherry, ¼ cup (2 fl oz/60 ml)

Worcestershire sauce, 1 tablespoon

Fresh tarragon, 1 tablespoon chopped

SERVES 4

italian
meatloaf

Ground (minced) beef chuck, ¾ lb (375 g)

Ground (minced) pork, ¾ lb (375 g)

Pesto, ½ cup (4 fl oz/ 125 ml)

Fine fresh bread crumbs, 1 cup (2 oz/60 g)

Oil-packed sun-dried tomatoes, ⅔ cup chopped

Egg, 1

Salt

SERVES 4–6

1 Mix the meatloaf

Preheat the oven to 350°F (180°C). Have ready an 11-by-7-inch (28-by-18-cm) shallow baking dish. In a large bowl, combine the beef, pork, pesto, bread crumbs, sun-dried tomatoes, egg, and ½ teaspoon salt. Mix gently but thoroughly with your hands. Form the mixture into a rough 9-by-5-inch (23-by-13-cm) loaf in the dish, then smooth the top.

2 Bake the meatloaf

Bake until the loaf is firm, the top is richly browned, and an instant-read thermometer inserted into the center registers 160°F (71°C). Let the loaf stand in the pan for 5–10 minutes before slicing. Divide slices among dinner plates and serve warm.

cook's tip

Leftover meatloaf makes great sandwiches. Spread slices of French or Italian bread with pesto-flavored mayonnaise, and layer each sandwich with slices of meatloaf and ripe tomatoes, topped with greens.

cook's tip

Serve this hearty pork dish
with the same wine that you
used to make it. A good rule
of thumb is to never use wine
to cook with that you would
not want to drink. Also, avoid
cooking with liquid labeled
"cooking wine," or the overall
flavor of your dish will suffer.

tuscan porchetta

1 Prepare the roast
Preheat the oven to 400°F (200°C). Finely grate 1 tablespoon zest from 1 of the lemons, then thinly slice the second lemon. Season the pork generously with the salt and pepper and the lemon zest, then sprinkle with the fennel seeds, patting them firmly so they adhere to the meat.

2 Roast the pork
In a shallow roasting pan just large enough to hold the pork, mix together the onion, fennel, and lemon slices, forming a bed for the meat. Sprinkle with salt and pepper and drizzle with 1/3 cup (2 1/2 fl oz/75 ml) of the wine. Place the pork on the bed of vegetables and lemon slices. Roast until an instant-read thermometer inserted into the center registers 145°–150°F (63°–65°C) and the pork is barely pink in the center, about 1 1/2 hours. Transfer the pork to a carving board, cover loosely with aluminum foil, and let stand for 10 minutes while you make the sauce.

3 Make the sauce
Meanwhile, place the roasting pan on the stovetop over medium heat, add the remaining 1/3 cup wine to the vegetables, and cook, stirring to scrape up the browned bits from the pan bottom, until slightly thickened, about 2 minutes. Snip the strings and cut the pork into slices. Arrange on a platter with the vegetables and sauce, and serve.

Lemons, 2

Boneless pork loin, 3 lb (1.5 kg), rolled and tied

Salt and freshly ground pepper

Fennel seeds, 2 teaspoons crushed

Yellow onion, 1, thinly sliced

Fennel bulb, 1, trimmed and thinly sliced

Dry white wine, 2/3 cup (5 fl oz/150 ml)

SERVES 6

ale-braised sausages & red cabbage

Olive oil, 2 tablespoons

German sausages, 4 large
or 8 small, 1 lb (500 g)

Yellow onion, 1, thinly sliced

Caraway seeds, 2 teaspoons

Red cabbage, ½ small head,
shredded

Amber ale, 1 cup
(8 fl oz/250 ml)

Malt vinegar, 2 tablespoons

Fresh dill, 2 tablespoons
chopped (optional)

SERVES 4

1 Brown the sausages and onion

In a large frying pan over medium-high heat, warm the
oil. Add the sausages and brown, turning once or twice,
until lightly charred, about 5 minutes. Transfer the sausages
to a plate. Add the onion to the pan, reduce the heat
to medium, and sauté until softened and lightly browned,
5–6 minutes. Stir in the caraway seeds, and then the
cabbage. Return the sausages and any juices from the plate
to the pan.

2 Braise the sausages and cabbage

Stir in the ale and vinegar and bring to a simmer. Cover,
reduce the heat to medium-low, and simmer until the cabbage
is tender, about 20 minutes. Stir in the dill, if using. Divide the
cabbage and sausages among dinner plates, and serve.

cook's tip

Any sausage can be used for this recipe. Kielbasa is already cooked so only brief warming is needed. Cut it into 2-inch (5-cm) pieces, cook over medium heat until browned and heated through, and add it to the cabbage during the last 10 minutes of cooking.

cook's tip

Paprika comes in a variety of
heat levels, and both smoked
(most often Spanish) and
unsmoked. For this recipe, use
unsmoked hot paprika, rather
than sweet or medium strength.
Once you have opened a new
paprika container, store it in
a cool, dark cupboard and use
within 6 months, as it loses
its pungency.

portuguese pork stew

1 Brown the pork

Season the pork generously with salt and pepper, then sprinkle with the paprika and cumin seeds, patting them firmly into the meat. In a large, deep frying pan or Dutch oven over medium-high heat, warm the oil. Working in batches, if needed, to avoid crowding, add the pork and cook, turning as needed, until browned on all sides, 6–8 minutes total. Using a slotted spoon, transfer the pork to a plate. Reduce heat to medium, add the onion and garlic to the pan and sauté until softened, 4–5 minutes. Stir in the wine and the broth, and return the pork and any juices from the plate to the pan.

2 Cook the stew

Bring the stew to a simmer, then cover the pan, reduce the heat to medium-low, and cook, stirring occasionally, for 1 hour. Add the sweet potatoes and carrots, re-cover, and continue to cook until the meat and vegetables are tender, about 30 minutes longer. Season to taste with salt and pepper. Divide among shallow bowls, and serve.

Boneless pork shoulder, 1 ½ lb (750 g), cut into 1 ½-inch (4-cm) chunks

Salt and freshly ground pepper

Hot paprika, 2 teaspoons

Cumin seeds, 2 teaspoons

Olive oil, 3 tablespoons

Red onion, 1, sliced

Garlic cloves, 4 large, minced

Full-bodied red wine, 1 cup (8 fl oz/250 ml)

Chicken broth, 2 cups (16 fl oz/500 ml)

Sweet potatoes, 1 lb (500 g), peeled and cut into 1-inch (2.5-cm) chunks

Carrots, 3 large, peeled and cut into 1-inch (2.5-cm) chunks

SERVES 4–6

arroz
con pollo

Bone-in, skin on chicken thighs, breast halves, and/ or drumsticks, 3 lb (1.5 kg)

Salt and freshly ground pepper

Olive oil, 3 tablespoons

Yellow onion, 1, chopped

Roasted red bell peppers (capsicums), 3, cut into thick strips

Garlic, 4 large cloves, minced

Saffron threads, ¼ teaspoon crushed

Long grain white rice, 2 cups (14 oz/440 g)

Chicken broth, 3 cups (24 fl oz/750 ml)

Fresh oregano, 2 tablespoons chopped

Diced tomatoes, 1 can (14½ oz/455 g), with juice

SERVES 4–6

1 Brown the chicken and vegetables

Preheat the oven to 350°F (180°C). Season the chicken generously with salt and pepper. In a large ovenproof frying pan with a tight fitting lid over medium-high heat, warm the oil. Add the chicken and cook, turning once or twice, until golden brown on both sides, about 6 minutes total. Transfer the chicken to a plate. Add the onion, roasted peppers, and garlic to the drippings in the pan, reduce the heat to medium, and sauté until the vegetables are softened, 4–5 minutes.

2 Cook the chicken and rice

Stir the saffron into the vegetables, then add the rice, stirring to coat all the grains. Stir in the broth and the oregano. Bring to a simmer. Return the chicken and any juices from the plate to the pan. Cover and bake for 45 minutes. Uncover and stir in the tomatoes. Cover and continue to cook until the rice is tender and most of the liquid is absorbed, about 15 minutes longer. Season to taste with salt and pepper. Serve directly from the pan.

cook's tip

For a quick paella, use
3 tablespoons chopped fresh
marjoram in place of the
oregano, substitute ½ cup
(4 fl oz/125 ml) dry white wine
for an equal amount of the broth,
and stir in 1 cup (5 oz/155 g)
frozen peas with the tomatoes.
You can also add Manila clams,
shrimp (prawns), or sliced
Spanish chorizo during the last
10 minutes of cooking.

balsamic beef stew

1 Brown the meat

In a resealable plastic bag, combine the flour and ½ teaspoon each salt and pepper. Add the beef, seal the bag, and shake to coat the beef with the seasoned flour. In a heavy pot or Dutch oven over medium-high heat, warm the oil. Working in batches, if needed, to avoid crowding, remove the beef from the bag, shaking off the excess flour, and add to the pot in a single layer. Cook, turning as needed, until browned on all sides, 6–8 minutes total. Using a slotted spoon, transfer the meat to a plate. Add the onion to the drippings in the pan and sauté over medium heat, until golden, about 5 minutes. Stir in the bay leaves, wine, and broth.

2 Braise the meat and vegetables

Return the meat and any juices from the plate to the pot. Bring to a simmer, then reduce the heat to low. Cover and braise until the meat is nearly fork-tender, 1½–2 hours. Add the potatoes and carrots, re-cover, and continue to braise until vegetables are tender, about 30 minutes more.

3 Finish the dish

Season the stew with salt and pepper. Remove and discard the bay leaves. Stir in the vinegar, divide among individual shallow bowls and serve.

Flour, 3 tablespoons

Salt and freshly ground pepper

Boneless beef chuck, 2 lb (1 kg) trimmed of excess fat and cut into 1½-inch (4-cm) pieces

Canola oil, 3 tablespoons

Red onion, 1 large, sliced

Bay leaves, 2

Full-bodied red wine, 1 cup (8 fl oz/250 ml)

Beef broth, 2 cups (16 fl oz/ 500 ml)

Red or Yukon gold potatoes, 1lb (500 g), unpeeled, cut into 1½-inch (4-cm) chunks

Carrots, 3 large, peeled and cut into 1-inch (2.5-cm) chunks

Balsamic vinegar, 2 tablespoons

SERVES 6

chicken korma

Boneless chicken thighs, 1½ lb (750 g), cut into 1-inch (2.5-cm) chunks

Salt and freshly ground pepper

Canola oil, 3 tablespoons

Yellow onion, 1, sliced

Garlic, 2 large cloves, minced

Ginger, 2 tablespoons finely chopped

Tomato sauce, ½ cup (4 fl oz/125 ml)

Chicken broth, ⅔ cup (5 fl oz/150 ml)

Plain whole-milk yogurt, ⅔ cup (5 oz/155 g)

Garam masala, 2 teaspoons

Fresh cilantro (fresh coriander), 3 tablespoons chopped

Basmati rice, for serving, (optional)

Roasted cashews, ½ cup (2½ oz/75 g), coarsely chopped

SERVES 4

1 Brown the chicken

Season the chicken generously with salt and pepper. In a large, deep frying pan over medium-high heat, warm the oil. Add the chicken and cook, turning once or twice, until golden brown on both sides, 5–7 minutes total. Using a slotted spoon, transfer the chicken to a plate.

2 Cook the vegetables

Add the onion to the drippings in the pan and sauté until softened, 4–5 minutes. Stir in the garlic and ginger and sauté until softened, about 1 minute. Stir in the tomato sauce and broth.

3 Finish the dish

Return the chicken and any juices from the plate to the pan, spooning the liquid over the chicken. Bring to a simmer, cover, reduce the heat to medium-low, and simmer, stirring once or twice, until the chicken is opaque throughout, 20–25 minutes. Remove from the heat and stir in the yogurt, garam masala, and 2 tablespoons of the cilantro. Divide the rice, if using, among shallow bowls and top with the chicken mixture. Sprinkle with the cashews and the remaining 1 tablespoon cilantro, and serve.

cook's tip

Be sure to use plain whole-milk yogurt for this recipe. Fat-free yogurt is not as substantial and will curdle and/or cause the sauce

to separate once it is mixed with the hot liquid, making for an unpleasant flavor as well as texture.

cook's tip

For a complete meal, serve the skewers over scallion rice. Cook rice according to package directions and stir in ¼ cup thinly sliced green (spring) onions and 1 tablespoon toasted sesame seeds.

grilled thai beef skewers

1 Marinate the beef

Cut the flank steak across the grain into slices ¼ inch (6 mm) thick. In a shallow glass or ceramic dish just large enough to hold the meat, stir together the sake, soy sauce, vinegar, honey, sesame oil, ginger, garlic, red pepper flakes, and coriander. Add the flank steak and stir to coat thoroughly. Cover and let stand for 30 minutes at room temperature or up to 4 hours in the refrigerator.

2 Prepare the skewers and grill

While the steak is marinating, soak 12 bamboo skewers in cold water for at least 30 minutes. Prepare a gas or charcoal grill for direct-heat grilling over high heat and oil the grill rack. Or, preheat a broiler (grill).

3 Cook the beef

Drain the skewers. Remove the meat from the marinade, discarding the marinade. Thread the meat onto the skewers, dividing the meat evenly. Place the skewers on the grill rack, or put on a rimmed baking sheet and place under the broiler. Cook, turning once or twice, until seared, 3–4 minutes total for medium-rare, or until done to your liking. Divide the skewers among dinner plates and serve.

Flank steak, 1 ½ lb (750 g)

Sake, dry sherry, or mirin, ⅓ cup (2 ½ fl oz/75 ml)

Soy sauce, ¼ cup (2 fl oz/ 60 ml)

Rice vinegar, ¼ cup (2 fl oz/ 60 ml)

Honey, 1 tablespoon

Asian sesame oil, 1 tablespoon

Ginger, 2 tablespoons finely chopped

Garlic, 3 cloves, minced

Red pepper flakes, 1 teaspoon

Ground coriander, ½ teaspoon

SERVES 4

oven-fried chicken

Lemon, 1

Buttermilk, ¾ cup
(6 fl oz/180 ml)

Fresh marjoram,
3 tablespoons chopped

**Salt and freshly ground
pepper**

Whole chicken, 1, 3 lb
(1.5 kg), skin intact and cut
into 10 serving pieces

Cornmeal, ⅔ cup
(3½ oz/105 g)

Fine dried bread crumbs,
⅓ cup (1½ oz/45 g)

Parmesan cheese, ¼ cup
(1 oz/30 g) grated

Unsalted butter,
4 tablespoons (2 oz/60 g),
melted

SERVES 4–6

1 **Soak the chicken**
Preheat the oven to 425°F (220°C). Grate 1 teaspoon zest and squeeze 2 tablespoons juice from the lemon. In a shallow glass or ceramic dish, stir together the buttermilk, lemon juice, 1 tablespoon of the marjoram, and about ¼ teaspoon each salt and pepper. Add the chicken pieces, turn to coat, and let stand for 10 minutes.

2 **Coat the chicken**
In a shallow bowl, stir together the cornmeal, bread crumbs, cheese, lemon zest, the remaining 2 tablespoons marjoram, and about ½ teaspoon each salt and pepper. One piece at a time, remove the chicken from the buttermilk and dip into the cornmeal mixture, turning to coat evenly. Arrange the pieces, skin side up and in a single layer, in a shallow roasting pan. Drizzle with the butter.

3 **Cook the chicken**
Place in the oven and cook until the chicken is crisp, browned, and opaque throughout, 35–45 minutes. Transfer to a platter, and serve.

cook's tip

The barbecue sauce can be
made up to 2 days in advance
and stored in an airtight
container in the refrigerator.
This versatile sauce is also
excellent on grilled chicken,
baby back ribs, or beef ribs.

spicy spareribs

1 **Make the sauce**
Preheat the oven to 350°F (180°C). In a saucepan over medium heat, warm the oil. Add the garlic and sauté until softened, about 1 minute. Stir in the tomatoes, molasses, bourbon, vinegar, Worcestershire sauce, chipotle chiles, cinnamon and salt and pepper to taste. Bring just to a boil, reduce the heat to medium-low, and simmer, uncovered, until moderately thick, 15–20 minutes.

2 **Roast the ribs**
Meanwhile, cut the ribs into serving-sized pieces of 3 ribs each. Arrange the ribs on a rack in a roasting pan large enough to hold them comfortably. Pour 2 cups (16 fl oz/500 ml) water into the pan. Cover the pan with heavy-duty aluminum foil. Roast the ribs for 35 minutes, then raise the oven heat to 375°F (190°C). Uncover the pan and brush the ribs on both sides with the sauce. Continue to roast, uncovered, for 15 minutes. Brush the ribs again and continue to roast until the ribs are tender, about 10 minutes longer, for a total roasting time of about 1 hour. Divide the ribs among dinner plates, passing additional sauce at the table.

Canola oil, 1 tablespoon

Garlic, 2 large cloves, minced

Diced tomatoes in purée, 1 can (14½ oz/455 g)

Molasses, ¼ cup (2½ oz/ 75 g)

Bourbon, or apple cider, 3 tablespoons

Cider vinegar, 2 tablespoons

Worcestershire sauce, 1 tablespoon

Chipotle chiles in adobo, 1 tablespoon finely chopped

Ground cinnamon, ¼ teaspoon

Salt and freshly ground pepper

Pork spareribs, 6 lb (3 kg)

SERVES 6

lamb tagine with apricots & almonds

Lemon, 1 large

Boneless lamb from leg,
2 lb (1 kg), cut into 2-inch
(5-cm) chunks

**Salt and freshly ground
pepper**

Olive oil, 3 tablespoons

Yellow onion, 1 large,
chopped

Garlic, 3 large cloves, minced

Ground coriander,
1 ½ teaspoons

Ground cumin,
1 ½ teaspoons

Ground cinnamon,
1 teaspoon

Chicken broth, 2 cups
(16 fl oz/500 ml)

**Dried apricots or pitted
dates, or a mixture,** ¾ cup
(4 oz/125 g), coarsely
chopped

Slivered almonds, ½ cup,
toasted

SERVES 6

1 Prepare the lemon zest and juice
Using a vegetable peeler, remove the zest in long wide strips from the lemon and then squeeze 1 ½ tablespoons juice. Reserve the zest and juice.

2 Brown the lamb
Season the lamb generously with salt and pepper. In a Dutch oven or deep, heavy frying pan over medium-high heat, warm the oil. Working in batches if necessary to avoid crowding, add the lamb and cook, turning as needed, until browned on all sides, 6–8 minutes total. Using a slotted spoon, transfer the lamb to a plate. Add the onion and garlic to the pan, reduce the heat to medium, and sauté until the onion is softened and lightly browned, 4–5 minutes. Stir in the coriander, cumin, and cinnamon. Return the lamb and any juices from the plate to the pan and stir to coat with the spices. Stir in the broth and bring to a simmer.

3 Braise the tagine
Cover, reduce the heat to low, and cook for 1 hour. Uncover, stir in the apricots, almonds, and lemon zest and juice and continue to simmer, uncovered, until the lamb is very tender and the liquids are lightly thickened to a sauce, about 20 minutes longer. Remove and discard the lemon zest, and season to taste with salt and pepper. Transfer to dinner plates or shallow bowls, and serve.

cook's tip

This Moroccan-inspired dish is delicious spooned over freshly steamed couscous. Boxes of quick-cooking couscous are carried in most markets. Serve it plain, or mix in some chopped fresh cilantro (fresh coriander).

make more
to store

pan-seared chicken with mustard sauce

PAN-SEARED CHICKEN

Skinless, boneless chicken breast halves, 8, about 3 lb (1.5 kg) total weight

Salt and freshly ground pepper

Unsalted butter, 6 tablespoons (3 oz/90 g)

Mustard seeds, 1 teaspoon

Dry white wine, ⅓ cup (3 fl oz/80 ml)

Chicken broth, ⅓ cup (3 fl oz/80 ml)

Heavy (double) cream, ¼ cup (2 fl oz/60 ml)

Dijon mustard, 2 tablespoons

SERVES 4

makes about 8 cups (2½ lb/1.25 kg) diced or shredded chicken total

Easy and quick, seared chicken breasts are served with a rich pan sauce the first night. The additional chicken can be used for making one of the hearty salads or flavorful wraps on the following pages.

1 Cook the chicken

Place the chicken between 2 sheets of waxed paper. Using a meat pounder or the flat bottom of a heavy pan, lightly pound the chicken until it is about ½ inch (12 mm) thick. Season generously with salt and pepper. In a large frying pan over medium-high heat, melt half of the butter. Add 4 breasts and cook, turning once, until golden on both sides and opaque throughout, 8–10 minutes total. Transfer the chicken to a plate to cool for storage (see Storage Tip). In the same pan, melt the remaining butter and cook the remaining chicken. Transfer to a separate plate.

2 Make the sauce

Stir the mustard seeds into the pan drippings over medium-high heat and cook, stirring, for about 15 seconds. Add the wine and broth and bring to a simmer. Reduce the heat to medium and cook, stirring, until slightly reduced, 1–2 minutes. Stir in the cream and mustard and cook for 1 minute to blend the flavors.

3 Finish the dish

Return 4 of the chicken breast halves and any juices to the pan and simmer over medium heat, about 1 minute. Season to taste with salt and pepper. Slice the chicken and divide among dinner plates. Drizzle with the sauce, and serve.

storage tip

To store the 4 remaining whole
chicken breast halves for use
in the following recipes, let them
cool to room temperature, then
place them in a resealable bag
or airtight container. They will
keep in the refrigerator for up
to 3 days. It's best not to freeze
poultry or meat once it has
been cooked.

cook's tip

You may use ¾ lb (12 oz/375 g)
skinless, boneless, cooked turkey
breast in place of the chicken.
For a light summertime supper,
serve the salad atop leaves of
green-leaf lettuce with a basket
of warm buttermilk biscuits.

chutney chicken
& pistachio salad

1 Make the dressing
Grate 1 teaspoon zest and squeeze 1 tablespoon juice from the lemon into a large bowl. Add the mayonnaise, chutney, and mustard, and stir to combine.

2 Assemble the salad
Add the chicken, grapes, celery, onion, and pistachios to the dressing. Stir gently to combine all the ingredients. Season to taste with salt and pepper. Divide among salad plates or bowls and serve.

Pan-Seared Chicken (page 70), 2 cups (12 oz/375 g) diced

Lemon, 1

Mayonnaise, ½ cup (4 fl oz/125 ml)

Mango chutney, ¼ cup (2½ oz/75 g)

Dijon mustard, 1 tablespoon

Seedless red grapes, 1 cup (6 oz/185 g), halved

Celery, 2–3 stalks, roughly chopped

Red onion, 1 small, finely chopped

Pistachios, ⅓ cup (2 oz/60 g)

Salt and freshly ground pepper

SERVES 4

vietnamese chicken salad

Pan-Seared Chicken (page 70), 2 cups (12 oz/375 g) shredded

Lime, 1 large

Peanut oil, 6 tablespoons (3 fl oz/90 ml)

Asian fish sauce, 2 tablespoons

Sugar, 1 tablespoon

Napa cabbage, 2 cups (6 oz/185 g) shredded or thinly sliced

Green (spring) onions, 4, thinly sliced

Fresh cilantro (fresh coriander), ¼ cup (⅓ oz/10 g) chopped

Salt and freshly ground pepper

Roasted peanuts, ¼ cup (1½ oz/45 g) coarsely chopped

SERVES 4

1 **Make the vinaigrette**
Grate 1 teaspoon zest and squeeze 2 tablespoons juice from the lime into a small bowl. Add the oil, fish sauce, and sugar and whisk together.

2 **Assemble the salad**
In a large bowl, combine the chicken, cabbage, green onions, and cilantro and toss to mix well. Drizzle on the lime vinaigrette and toss to coat all the ingredients. Season to taste with salt and pepper. Divide among salad plates, top with the peanuts, and serve.

cook's tip

To turn this salad into a heartier
main course, add 8 oz (250 g)
cooked rice vermicelli noodles
along with the chicken and
cabbage and toss to coat well
with the vinaigrette.

cook's tip

Sandwiches and wraps are
ideal for using up leftovers.
Experiment with different
combinations such as sliced
leftover steak (page 86),
horseradish mayonnaise, and
sliced ripe tomatoes.

tarragon chicken & avocado wrap

1 Make the dressing
Finely grate 1 teaspoon zest and squeeze
1½ tablespoons juice from the lemon into a bowl. Add
the mayonnaise and tarragon and stir to combine.

2 Assemble the chicken salad
Add the chicken and avocado to the dressing and
toss gently to coat all the ingredients. Season to taste
with salt and pepper.

3 Assemble the wraps
On a work surface, lay out the lavash. Divide the
chicken salad equally among the 4 lavash, spreading almost
to the edges. Tear the watercress into small sprigs and scatter
over the chicken salad. Fold the left and right sides over the
filling about 1 inch (2.5 cm) on each side, then starting at the
bottom, roll each into cylinders, enclosing the filling, and serve.

**Pan-Seared Chicken
(page 70),** 2 cups
(12 oz/375 g) diced

Lemon, 1

Mayonnaise ½ cup
(4 fl oz/125 ml)

Fresh tarragon,
2 tablespoons chopped

Avocado, 1, halved, pitted,
peeled, and coarsely chopped

**Salt and freshly ground
pepper**

**Soft lavash or 8-inch
(20-cm) flour tortillas,** 4

**Watercress or arugula
(rocket),** 1 small bunch,
tough stems removed

SERVES 4

roast pork loin with pan sauce

ROAST PORK

Boneless pork loin, 4 lb
(2 kg), rolled and tied

Garlic, 1 large clove, halved

**Salt and freshly ground
pepper**

Butter, 3 tablespoons

Flour, 1 tablespoon

Dry white wine, ¼ cup
(2 fl oz/60 ml)

Chicken broth, ¼ cup
(2 fl oz/60 ml)

SERVES 4

makes about 4 cups
(3½ lb/1.75 kg) shredded
or thinly sliced roast pork
total

Readying this pork roast for the oven takes fewer than 5 minutes. Serve slices with pan sauce on the first night, then use the leftovers for making the recipes on the following pages later in the week.

1 **Prepare the pork**
Preheat the oven to 450°F (230°C). Pat the pork dry with paper towels, then rub it all over with the cut sides of the garlic clove. Sprinkle with 2 teaspoons each salt and pepper.

2 **Roast the pork**
Place the pork, fat side up, on a rack in a shallow roasting pan just large enough to hold it comfortably. Roast for 15 minutes. Reduce the temperature to 400°F (200°C) and continue to roast until an instant-read thermometer inserted into the center registers 145°–150°F (63°–65°C) and the pork is barely pink in the center, 1–1¼ hours longer. Transfer the pork to a carving board, tent with aluminum foil, and let stand for 10 minutes.

3 **Prepare the pan sauce**
While the pork is resting, remove the rack from the roasting pan and place the pan on the stovetop over medium heat. Add the butter and stir with a whisk to scrape up the browned bits in the pan. Sprinkle in the flour, and cook, stirring for about 2 minutes. Add the wine and broth and stir until smooth and thick. Snip the strings and slice enough pork for one meal. Serve the pork drizzled with the pan sauce. Let the remaining pork cool, then store for later use (see Storage Tip).

storage tip

To store the remaining pork loin for use in the following recipes, let it cool to room temperature, then wrap it tightly in plastic wrap. The pork loin will stay juicier if you store it whole rather than in slices. It will keep in the refrigerator for up to 2 days.

cook's tip

Vietnamese sandwiches are
traditionally made ahead
of time and wrapped tightly
in plastic wrap, allowing
the flavors to come together.
You can assemble and wrap
them up to 4 hours in advance
and refrigerate.

vietnamese-style pork sandwich

1 **Marinate the pork**
In a small bowl, toss the pork with the soy sauce, garlic, and fish sauce. Let stand for 5 minutes.

2 **Assemble the sandwiches**
Spread the cut sides of the baguette with the mayonnaise. Layer the pork, cucumber, carrots, onion, chile, and cilantro on the bottom half of the baguette. Close the sandwich with the top half of the baguette and cut on the diagonal into 4 individual sandwiches.

Roast Pork (page 78), 2 cups (12 oz/375 g) very thinly sliced

Soy sauce, 2 tablespoons

Garlic, 1 large clove, minced

Fish sauce, 2 teaspoons

Baguette, 1, about 24 inches (60 cm) long, split lengthwise

Mayonnaise, 1/4 cup (2 fl oz/ 60 ml)

Cucumber, 1 small, peeled and thinly sliced lengthwise

Carrots, 2, peeled and thinly sliced or shredded

Red onion, 1 small, thinly sliced

Jalapeño chile, 1, seeded and thinly sliced or minced

Fresh cilantro (fresh coriander), 1/4 cup (1/3 oz/ 10 g) chopped

SERVES 4

tortilla soup
with pork

Roast Pork (page 78),
1 ½ cups (9 oz/280 g)
shredded

Corn oil, 2 tablespoons

Red onion, 1 small, chopped

Garlic, 2 large cloves, minced

Chipotle chiles in adobo,
1 tablespoon finely chopped

Chicken broth, 6 cups
(48 fl oz/1.5 l)

Diced tomatoes, 1 can
(14½ oz/455 g), with juice

**Fresh cilantro (fresh
coriander),** 4 tablespoons
(⅓ oz/10 g) chopped

Queso fresco, ½ cup
(2 oz/60 g) crumbled

Avocado, 1 small, halved,
pitted, peeled, and finely diced

Tortilla chips, 1 cup
(3 oz/ 90 g) broken

Lime, 1, cut into wedges

SERVES 4

1 Make the soup base
In a large saucepan over medium heat, warm the oil. Add the onion and garlic and sauté until the onion is softened, 4–5 minutes. Stir in the chile, broth, and tomatoes, then stir in the pork. Raise the heat to medium-high and bring to a simmer. Reduce the heat to medium-low, cover partially, and simmer for 10 minutes to blend the flavors.

2 Finish the soup
Stir 2 tablespoons of the cilantro into the soup. Ladle into bowls and sprinkle with the remaining 2 tablespoons cilantro and the cheese, avocado, and tortilla chips. Accompany with the lime wedges.

cook's tip

You can also garnish this flavorful soup with a dollop of sour cream, tomatillo salsa, or a spoonful of black beans. Instead of queso fresco, use shredded Monterey jack cheese. For a complete meal, accompany the soup with a chopped romaine (cos) lettuce salad with a chile-lime vinaigrette.

cook's tip

Fresh lo mein or chow mein
noodles can be used in place
of commercial dried noodles.
Fresh noodles will cook in just
a few minutes, or according
to the package directions.

pork
lo mein

1 Cook the noodles
Bring a large pot of water to a boil. Add 1 tablespoon salt and the noodles. Cook, stirring occasionally to prevent sticking, until the noodles are al dente, according to the package directions. Drain well and reserve.

2 Make the sauce
Meanwhile, in a frying pan or saucepan over medium heat, warm the oil. Add the garlic and carrots and stir to incorporate, about 30 seconds. Stir in the broth, soy sauce, oyster sauce, and sherry. Add the pork, bring to a simmer, reduce the heat to medium-low, and cook, uncovered, for about 5 minutes.

3 Assemble the lo mein
Add the noodles to the pan, sprinkle with the green onions, and toss well to combine. Season with salt to taste, and serve directly from the pan.

Roast Pork (page 78),
2 cups (12 oz/375 g)
shredded

Salt

**Dried lo mein noodles
or spaghetti,** ¾ lb (375 g)

Asian sesame oil,
3 tablespoons

Garlic, 3 large cloves, minced

Carrots, 2, peeled, halved
lengthwise, and thinly sliced
crosswise

Chicken broth, ¾ cup
(6 fl oz/180 ml)

Soy sauce, 2 tablespoons

Oyster sauce, 2 tablespoons

Dry sherry, 1 tablespoon

Green (spring) onions,
4, white and pale green
parts only, thinly sliced

SERVES 4

grilled tri-tip & vegetables

GRILLED TRI-TIP

Tri-tip roasts, 2, about 2 lb (1 kg) each

Salt and freshly ground pepper

Zucchini (courgette), 1, sliced lengthwise about ¼ inch (6 mm) thick

Eggplant (aubergine), 1 small, sliced lengthwise about ¼ inch (6 mm) thick

Orange or yellow bell pepper (capsicum), 1, seeded and quartered lengthwise

Sweet onion such as Vidalia, 1 small, sliced crosswise about ¼ inch (6 mm) thick

Olive oil, ¼ cup (2 fl oz/60 ml)

Fresh rosemary, 1 tablespoon chopped (optional)

SERVES 4–6

makes about 6 cups (3½ lb/1.75 g) thinly sliced beef total

Tri-tip, a lean, flavorful cut from the bottom sirloin, is perfect for the grill. Serve one tri-tip with the smoky grilled vegetables, and use the second one for making the recipes on the following pages.

1 Prepare the tri-tip and vegetables

Prepare a gas or charcoal grill for direct-heat grilling over medium-high heat or preheat the broiler (grill). Season the tri-tip generously with salt and pepper. Let stand at room temperature for 10 minutes. Brush the zucchini, eggplant, bell pepper, and onion with the oil. Sprinkle with the rosemary and season with salt and pepper.

2 Grill the tri-tip

Place the tri-tip over the hottest part of the fire or under the broiler (grill). Cover the grill and cook, turning once or twice with tongs, for about 30 minutes total for medium-rare, or until cooked to your liking. Transfer 1 roast to a carving board and let stand 5–10 minutes before slicing. Set the second roast aside to cool, then store for later use (see Storage Tip).

3 Grill the vegetables

While the tri-tip is resting, place the vegetables on the grill rack, away from the hottest part of the fire, or under the broiler. Grill, turning once or twice, until lightly charred and tender, 4–6 minutes. Transfer to a platter or to the edge of the grill to keep them warm. Thinly slice the tri-tip across the grain and serve with the vegetables.

storage tip

To store the second tri-tip for use in the following recipes, let it cool to room temperature, then wrap it, unsliced, in aluminum foil. It will keep in the refrigerator for up to 2 days. To reheat, place, wrapped, in a 300°F (150°C) oven for 15 minutes.

cook's tip

You can use 3–4 oil-packed
sun-dried tomatoes, drained
and cut into strips, in place
of the roasted peppers.

beef & goat cheese
sandwiches

1 Toast the bread

Preheat a broiler (grill). Arrange the bread slices on a rimmed baking sheet. Lightly toast the bread on one side, watching carefully to prevent burning, about 1 minute. Turn the bread, spread with the goat cheese, and top with the red peppers and beef and broil until the beef is warmed through, about 1 minute.

2 Assemble the sandwiches

While still hot, drizzle the open-faced sandwiches with the vinegar, sprinkle with the basil, and serve.

Grilled Tri-Tip (page 86),
2 cups (12 oz/375 g) thinly sliced

Crusty country bread,
8 slices

Soft fresh goat cheese,
¼ lb (125 g)

Roasted red bell peppers (capsicums), 4, sliced

Balsamic vinegar,
1 tablespoon

Fresh basil leaves,
¼ cup (¼ oz/7 g) slivered

SERVES 4

beef stir-fry with black bean sauce

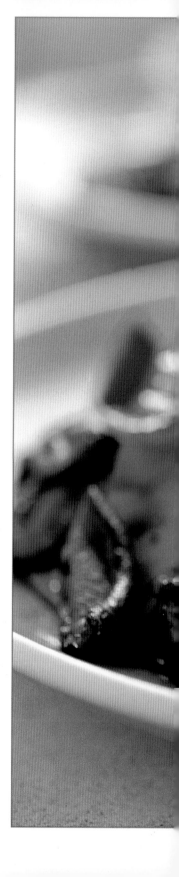

Grilled Tri-Tip (page 86), 2 cups (12 oz/375 g) thinly sliced and cut into strips

Peanut oil, 3 tablespoons

Red bell pepper (capsicum), 1 large, seeded and thinly sliced

Snow peas, 1 cup

Yellow onion, 1, thinly sliced

Shiitake mushrooms, ¼ lb (125 g), sliced

Red pepper flakes, ¼ teaspoon

Black bean sauce, ¼ cup (2 fl oz/60 ml)

Salt and freshly ground pepper

Steamed rice, for serving (optional)

SERVES 4

1 **Stir-fry the vegetables**
In a wok or large, deep frying pan over high heat, warm the oil. Add the bell pepper, snow peas, onion, mushrooms, and red pepper flakes and stir-fry until the vegetables are crisp-tender and lightly browned, 2–3 minutes.

2 **Finish the dish**
Stir in the black bean sauce and 2 tablespoons water, reduce the heat to medium-low, and simmer for 2 minutes. Stir in the beef and simmer until heated through, 1–2 minutes. Season to taste with salt and pepper and serve over rice.

cook's tip

This recipe can easily be made
into a soup. Add 2 cups (16 fl oz/
500 ml) chicken broth along
with the bean sauce and water in
Step 2. Simmer for 10 minutes
to blend flavors. Be sure to taste
and season both the stir-fry
and the soup just before serving.

cook's tip

This versatile Greek-inspired
salad can also be prepared with
rotisserie chicken in place of
the beef. Slice the chicken thinly
before adding to the salad.
Serve the salad with warm pita
bread and fresh pistachio
or walnut baklava for dessert.

greek-style beef salad

1 **Make the vinaigrette**
In a small bowl, whisk together the oil, lemon juice, 2 tablespoons of the mint, and the garlic. Season to taste with about ½ teaspoon each salt and pepper.

2 **Assemble the salad**
In a bowl, toss the watercress with about half of the vinaigrette. Arrange the beef, onion, cucumber, tomatoes, olives, and cheese on top of the watercress and gently toss. Divide among salad plates. Drizzle with the remaining vinaigrette, sprinkle with the remaining mint, and serve.

Grilled Tri-Tip (page 86), 2 cups (12 oz/375 g) thinly sliced

Olive oil, ½ cup (4 fl oz/ 125 ml)

Lemon juice, from 2 lemons

Fresh mint, 3 tablespoons chopped

Garlic, 1 large clove, minced

Salt and freshly ground pepper

Watercress, 1 large bunch, tough stems removed

Red onion, 1, halved lengthwise and thinly sliced

Cucumber, 1, halved lengthwise, seeded, and thinly sliced crosswise

Grape or cherry tomatoes, 1 cup (6 oz/186 g), halved

Kalamata or other Mediterranean black olives, ¾ cup (3½ oz/ 105 g), pitted

Feta cheese, ¼ lb (125 g), crumbled

SERVES 4

93

the smarter cook

Becoming a smarter cook means that you'll spend less time in the kitchen but still sit down to a delicious, wholesome home-cooked dinner every night. Start with a collection of tasty recipes and a few strategic shopping trips to stock the pantry and refrigerator. Come dinner time, you'll be able to vary your meals every night of the week in only 30 minutes or less of hands-on time.

Keep your pantry well stocked, and you'll have the foundation for all your weekday dinners. Plan weekly menus and make detailed shopping lists and you'll always be ready to cook. Roast a pork loin or grill a tri-tip on the weekend, and use the leftovers for meals during the week. In the following pages, you'll find dozens of tips on how to manage your time and organize your kitchen—the keys to becoming a smarter cook.

sample meals

These meals are divided into three categories to help you plan your weekly menus. Depending on your schedule, you can mix and match from the different columns. It is a smart idea to cook double portions of your favorite recipes on the weekend so you can enjoy the same dish again later in the week.

EASY WEEKNIGHT	SUNDAY SUPPER	FIT FOR COMPANY
Penne with Basil & Pine Nuts (page 18) Sliced tomatoes with balsamic vinegar & olive oil	**Portuguese Pork Stew** (page 53) Crusty bread Mixed greens with vinaigrette	**Lamb Tagine with Apricots & Almonds** (page 66) Couscous Orange, sweet onion & olive salad
Oven-Fried Chicken (page 62) Chive mashed potatoes Steamed broccoli with lemon butter	**Spicy Spareribs** (page 65) Coleslaw Corn on the cob	**Roast Pork Loin with Pan Sauce** (page 78) Roasted red potatoes Braised winter greens with garlic
Beef & Asparagus Stir-Fry (page 17) Steamed rice with cilantro (fresh coriander)	**Arroz con Pollo** (page 54) Avocado, tomato & red onion salad	**Chicken in Orange- Riesling Sauce** (page 10) Wild rice pilaf Sautéed broccoli rabe
Ale-Braised Sausages & Red Cabbage (page 50) Dark rye or pumpernickel bread Cucumber salad with dill	**Chile-Rubbed Pork with Corn Salsa** (page 22) Roasted sweet potato wedges Pinto beans	**Balsamic Beef Stew** (page 57) Buttered egg noodles Spinach salad with toasted pine nuts & vinaigrette
Pork Schnitzel with Arugula (page 14) Roasted sweet potato wedges	**Steak au Poivre** (page 30) Sautéed zucchini (courgettes) Garlic mashed potatoes	**Veal Piccata** (page 21) Herbed focaccia Sautéed green beans with herbs
Ginger Chicken & Green Onions (page 13) Steamed rice Sugar snap peas	**Braised Chicken, Tomatoes & Bacon** (page 42) Creamy polenta	

Prep ahead. Make a habit of prepping your ingredients the night before, whether it's chopping vegetables, pounding veal cutlets, preparing marinades, or skewering steak kebabs. Store ingredients in airtight containers in the refrigerator until needed.

Use the right tools. Good knives are indispensable to working efficiently in the kitchen. Start with an 8-inch (20-cm) chef's knife, a paring knife, a bread knife, and a knife sharpener. You also need a frying pan, a roasting pan with a rack, and several heavy-bottomed saucepans in an assortment of sizes.

Ready your ingredients. When you start a recipe, take out and measure all your ingredients. That way, you won't find yourself digging through the pantry in search of sesame seeds or cider vinegar at the last minute, and counters won't be cluttered with cartons and jars. Pick up a set of small nested bowls in graduated sizes for holding the ingredients.

Clean as you go. Keep your kitchen organized by cleaning up as you go. Start out with a clean kitchen and an empty dishwasher—and make sure you have clean dish towels on hand. Put away ingredients as you use them, wipe down your work surfaces frequently, and move used pans and bowls to the sink or dishwasher once you are done with them. Fill dirty pans with hot water to soak while you're eating, by the time you're back in the kitchen, any browned-on food will be easier to scrub off.

shortcut suppers

On the days when you don't have time to cook a meal from scratch, a well-stocked supermarket can provide lots of tasty, wholesome items to fill out your meal.

▥ **Rotisserie chicken** Buy enough chicken for two meals. On the first night, serve it accompanied with crusty bread and a simple salad. On another night, bone and skin the remaining chicken, shred the meat, and toss it with pasta and vegetables, or use it to make a chicken salad.

▥ **Cooked sausages** Keep fully cooked meat- or poultry-based sausages, such as chicken-apple, Italian, and kielbasa, in the refrigerator or freezer. Panfry the sausages until heated through and lightly browned, then slice lengthwise and serve with sautéed onions and peppers on warmed hero sandwich rolls or lengths of baguette.

▥ **Marinated kebabs** Most butcher shops and supermarkets sell premarinated beef, pork, and lamb skewers. Grill or broil the kebabs, then serve with warmed pita bread or quick-cooking couscous.

▥ **Frittata** Make sure there is a supply of eggs on hand for last-minute meals. For a quick main dish, sauté cooked, chopped vegetables or meats in olive oil in a frying pan until cooked or heated through. Add whisked eggs, salt, and pepper, and cook without stirring and lifting the edges to let the uncooked egg flow underneath, until almost set. Top with grated parmesan cheese and put under the pre-heated broiler (grill) for a minute or two until fully set and browned on top. Invert the pan over a plate, cut into wedges, and serve with a salad.

▥ **Quesadillas** Keep flour tortillas in the refrigerator for preparing quesadillas or tacos using cheese and leftover chicken, sausage slices, or vegetables. Stock up on salsa, rice, and canned refried, pinto, or black beans to round out the menu.

▥ **Open-faced sandwiches** Pile leftover meat or vegetables on slices of crusty bread to make open-faced sandwiches. Top with slices of fresh mozzarella or provolone and broil (grill) until the cheese melts.

shop smarter

Using high-quality, fresh ingredients will give you a head start toward great flavor and healthier eating. Look for a butcher, produce store, and market that you can rely on for first-rate goods and dependable service. Call ahead and place your order, so it's ready to pick up on your way home from work. Stop by your local farmers' market regularly for the freshest local produce and to keep up with what's in season.

■ **Produce** Look for locally grown produce whenever possible for better flavor and healthier eating. Items grown elsewhere have often been picked long before they ripen and rarely achieve peak flavor. Greens and herbs should be crisp and brightly colored, without dark edges or limp leaves. Root vegetables like carrots and beets should be hard, not flabby, and other vegetables, like cucumbers, eggplants (aubergines), and zucchini (courgettes), should be firm to the touch with taut skins. If you live near a regular farmers' market, get in the habit of visiting it once a week. You'll learn when specific items are in season, and you'll often find good deals on produce.

■ **Meat** Look for meat with good, uniform color and no sign of shriveling at the edge. Fat should be bright white rather than grayish, and the meat should have a fresh smell. It's a good idea ask your butcher to trim, grind, chop, or bone items as necessary, to save you time in the kitchen. Many butcher shops now carry organic and/or pasture-raised beef, pork, and lamb. Taste and compare what's offered to discover what tastes best to you. While much modern pork has been bred for leanness (often at the expense of moistness and tenderness), some specialty pork operations are returning to old-fashioned breeds whose meat can offer richer, more distinctive flavor. Ask your butcher if he or she carries pork from these heritage breeds.

■ **Poultry** Smooth skin, firm flesh, white to yellowish fat, and a fresh smell are the marks of quality poultry. A good butcher will be happy to cut up or debone a chicken or grind fresh turkey for you. Experiment with the different types of poultry available, such as kosher, organic, heritage breeds, and free range; and then buy what tastes best to you.

MAKE A SHOPPING LIST

prepare in advance Make a list of what you need to buy before you go shopping, and you'll save time.

make a template Create a list template, then fill it in during the week before you go shopping.

categorize your lists Use the following categories to keep your lists organized: pantry, fresh, and occasional.

■ **pantry items** Check the pantry and write down any items that need to be restocked to make the meals on your weekly plan.

■ **fresh ingredients** These are for immediate use and include produce, poultry, meats, and some cheeses. You may need to visit different stores or supermarket sections, so divide the list into subcategories, such as produce, dairy, and meats.

■ **occasional items** This is a list for refrigerated items that are replaced as needed, such as butter and eggs.

be flexible Be ready to change your menus based on the freshest ingredients at the market.

food processor This workhorse of the modern kitchen is good for chopping, grating, and shredding vegetables. A mini processor is useful for mincing a small amount of garlic or fresh herbs, while a standard model is handy for chopping onions, making pesto, and shredding cheese or carrots.

grill pan No time to fire up the grill? This heavy-bottomed, ridged pan is used on the stovetop and can yield seared, cross-hatched vegetables and meats that look and taste almost as if they were cooked on an outdoor grill. Always let the empty pan preheat over high heat for at least 5 minutes before adding the food.

salad spinner Wash and dry your greens using one handy implement. Whether your spinner uses a pump, crank, or pull cord, the centrifugal force whirling your greens will ensure a crisp, dry salad every time.

dried herbs Some dried herbs, including dried thyme, rosemary, and sage, can be used successfully when you don't have fresh herbs handy. Their flavor is more concentrated, however, so use only one-third to one-half the amount of fresh.

sharp knives You will prep your ingredients twice as fast if you don't have to struggle with a dull knife. It's a good idea to take a minute or two to sharpen a knife before you put it away, so it will be ready to use next time you cook.

make the most of your time

Once you've drawn up your weekly meal plan, you can begin thinking how to make the most of your time. Get your shopping and prep work done in advance, and you'll be ready to cook when dinnertime arrives.

▪ **Stock up.** Avoid last-minute shopping trips or missing ingredients by keeping your pantry well stocked. Make a note on your shopping list whenever you're getting low on any staple, and replace it promptly. Also keep a good supply of basic nonperishable ingredients on hand so you can improvise simple main and side dishes when needed.

▪ **Shop less.** Write out your shopping list as you plan your meals so you can pick up all the staples you'll need for the week in one trip. If you know that you'll be pressed for time during the week, purchase your meat and poultry along with your staples and wrap and freeze what you won't be using in the next couple of days.

▪ **Do it ahead.** Do as much as you can in advance when you have extra time. Wash, peel, and chop vegetables and store them in sealed plastic bags or airtight containers. Pound chicken or veal cutlets, wrap tightly with plastic wrap, and refrigerate. Prepare marinades or salad dressings and store in the refrigerator. Cook extra side dishes, such as rice, polenta, or steamed vegetables, and store in airtight containers until needed. Check your ingredients and tools the night before so you'll be able to find everything easily when you start to cook.

▪ **Double up.** Instead of serving a reheated version of the same dish the next night, double up the foundation of the meal. For example, roast two chickens or two pork tenderloins. Prepare one for tonight according to the recipe, and reserve the second for a hearty soup or salad the next night.

▪ **Cook smarter.** Read through the recipe from start to finish before you begin cooking. As you read, go through the recipe step by step in your mind and visualize all the techniques. If you have friends or family around, figure out how they can help, whether it's peeling carrots, making a salad, or setting the table.

the well-stocked kitchen

Organize and stock your pantry, refrigerator, and freezer, and you'll have a big head start on getting dinner on the table. If you're sure of what you have—and of what you need—in the kitchen, you'll make fewer trips to the grocery store and you'll spend less time when you're there.

In the following pages, you'll discover an easy-to-use guide to all the ingredients you'll need to make the recipes in this book. You'll also find plenty of tips on how to keep them fresh and properly stored. Go through your kitchen with these lists to see what you already have and what you'll need to buy or replace when you go shopping. Stock up and put your kitchen in order now, and you'll have more time to spend with family and friends around the table.

the pantry

Typically, the pantry is a closet or one or more cupboards where you store dried herbs and spices, canned and jarred condiments, oils and vinegars, grains and pastas, and such fresh foods as potatoes, onions, garlic, ginger, and shallots. Make sure your pantry is cool, dry, and dark when not in use, as direct heat or light can sap herbs and spices of their flavor and hasten spoilage of grains and oils.

stock your pantry

- Take inventory of what is in your pantry using the Pantry Staples list.

- Remove everything from the pantry; clean the shelves and line with paper, if needed; and then resort the items by type.

- Discard items that have passed their expiration date or have a stale or otherwise questionable appearance or odor.

- Make a list of items that you need to replace or stock.

- Shop for the items on your list.

- Restock the pantry, organizing items by type.

- Write the purchase date on perishable items and label bulk items.

- Keep staples you use often toward the front of the pantry.

- Keep dried herbs and spices in tightly sealed containers and preferably in a separate spice or herb organizer, shelf, or drawer.

keep it organized

- Look over the recipes in your weekly menu plan and check your pantry to make sure you have all the ingredients you'll need.

- Rotate items as you use them, moving the oldest ones to the front of the pantry so they will be used first.

- Keep a list of the items you use up so you can replace them.

PANTRY STORAGE

dried herbs & spices Dried herbs and spices start losing flavor after about 6 months, so buy in small quantities and replace often. Store in airtight containers.

oils Store unopened bottles of oil at room temperature in a cool, dark place. Oils will keep for up to 1 year, but their flavor diminishes over time. Store opened bottles for 3 months at room temperature or in the refrigerator for up to 6 months.

grains & pasta Store grains in airtight containers for up to 3 months. The shelf life of most dried pastas is 1 year. Although safe to eat beyond that time, they will have lost flavor. Once you open a package, put what you don't cook into an airtight container.

fresh foods Store in a cool, dark place and check occasionally for sprouting or spoilage. Don't put potatoes alongside onions; when placed next to each other, they produce gases that hasten spoilage.

canned foods Discard canned foods if the can shows signs of expansion or buckling. Once a can is opened, transfer the unused contents to an airtight container and refrigerate.

PANTRY STAPLES

GRAINS & PASTAS

basmati rice

cornmeal

couscous

dried bread crumbs

lo mein

long-grain white rice

penne

rice vermicelli noodles

spaghetti

FRESH FOODS

avocados

garlic

ginger

onions (red, sweet, yellow)

potatoes (red, sweet, white, Yukon gold)

shallots

tomatoes

SPIRITS

amber ale or dark beer

bourbon

brandy

Cognac

dry sherry

Marsala

mirin

Port

red wine, full bodied

sake

tequila

white wine, dry and fruity

OILS

Asian sesame oil

canola oil

corn oil

olive oil

peanut oil

VINEGARS

balsamic vinegar

cider vinegar

malt vinegar

red wine vinegar

rice vinegar

CONDIMENTS

Asian fish sauce

black bean sauce

Dijon mustard

hoisin sauce

honey mustard

mango chutney

mayonnaise

oyster sauce

soy sauce

Worcestershire sauce

NUTS & DRIED FRUITS

almonds

apricots

cashews

cherries

dates

peanuts

pistachios

DRIED HERBS & SPICES

ancho chile powder

bay leaves

black peppercorns

caraway seeds

cinnamon, ground & sticks

coriander, ground

cumin, ground

cumin seeds

garam masala

mustard seeds

paprika

red pepper flakes

saffron

sesame seeds

CANNED & JARRED FOODS

beef broth

chicken broth

capers

chipotle chiles in adobo

honey

Kalamata olives

oil-packed sun-dried tomatoes

pesto

roasted red peppers (capsicums)

tomatoes

MISCELLANEOUS

flour

molasses

sugar

tortillas

the refrigerator & freezer

Once you have stocked and organized your pantry, you can apply the same time-saving principles to your refrigerator and freezer. Used for short-term cold storage, the refrigerator is ideal for keeping meats, poultry, dairy, vegetables, and leftovers fresh. Proper freezing will preserve most of the flavor in meat, poultry, and many prepared dishes for several months.

general tips

- Foods lose flavor under refrigeration, so proper storage and an even temperature of below 40°F (5°C) is important.

- Freeze foods at 0°F (-18°C) or below to retain color, texture, and flavor.

- Don't crowd foods in the refrigerator. Air must circulate freely to keep foods evenly cooled.

- To prevent freezer burn, use only moistureproof wrappings, such as aluminum foil, airtight plastic containers, or resealable plastic bags.

leftover storage

- You can store most prepared main dishes in an airtight container in the refrigerator for up to 4 days or in the freezer for up to 4 months.

- Check the contents of the refrigerator at least once a week and promptly discard old or spoiled food.

- Let food cool to room temperature before storing in the refrigerator or freezer. Transfer the cooled food to an airtight plastic or glass container, leaving room for expansion if freezing. Or, put the cooled food into a resealable plastic bag, expelling as much air as possible before sealing.

- Freeze some main dishes in small portions for when you need to heat up just enough to serve one or two people.

- Thaw frozen leftovers in the refrigerator or in the microwave. To avoid bacterial contamination, never thaw at room temperature.

FREEZING & THAWING

- For the best flavor and texture, use frozen raw meat and poultry within 6 months of freezing.

- Label all packages or containers with the date and contents before putting them in the freezer.

- Always thaw frozen meat and poultry in the refrigerator, never at room temperature or by running them under warm or hot water.

KEEP IT ORGANIZED

clean first Remove items and wash the refrigerator thoroughly with warm, soapy water, then rinse well with clear water.

rotate items Check the expiration dates on refrigerated items and discard any that have exceeded their time.

date of purchase Label items that you plan to keep for more than a few weeks, writing the date directly on the package or on a piece of masking tape.

fresh herb & vegetable storage

▦ Trim the stem ends of a bunch of parsley, stand the bunch in a glass of water, drape a plastic bag loosley over the leaves, and refrigerate. Wrap other fresh herbs in a damp paper towel, slip into a plastic bag, and store in the crisper. Rinse and stem all herbs just before using.

▦ Store tomatoes and eggplants (aubergines) at room temperature.

▦ Cut about ½ inch (12 mm) off the end of each asparagus spear; stand the spears, tips up, in a glass of cold water, and refrigerate, changing the water daily. The asparagus will keep for up to 1 week.

▦ Rinse leafy greens, such as chard, spin dry in a salad spinner, wrap in damp paper towels, and store in a resealable plastic bag in the crisper for up to a week. In general, store other vegetables in resealable bags in the crisper and rinse before using. Sturdy vegetables will keep for up to a week; more delicate ones will keep for only a few days.

cheese storage

▦ Wrap all cheeses well to prevent them from drying out. Hard cheeses, such as Parmesan, have a low moisture content, so they keep longer than fresh cheeses, such as queso fresco. Use fresh cheeses within a couple of days. Store soft and semisoft cheeses, such as Fontina, for up to 2 weeks and hard cheeses up to 1 month.

meat & poultry storage

▦ Use fresh meat and poultry within 2 days of purchase. If using packaged meat, check the expiration date on the package and use before that date. Most seafood should be used the day of purchase.

▦ To prevent cross-contamination with other foods, always place packaged meats on a plate in the coldest part of the refrigerator. Once you have opened the package, discard original wrappings and rewrap any unused portions in fresh wrapping.

index

weldon**owen**

415 Jackson Street, Suite 200, San Francisco, CA 94111
www.wopublishing.com

MEALS IN MINUTES SERIES
Conceived and produced by Weldon Owen Inc.
Copyright © 2007 by Weldon Owen Inc. and Williams-Sonoma, Inc.

The recipes in this book have been previously published
as *Simple Suppers* in the Food Made Fast series.

Color separations by Mission Productions in China
Printed by 1010 Printing in China

Set in Formata
This edition first printed in 2011
10 9 8 7 6 5 4 3 2

Library of Congress Cataloging-in-Publication
data is available.

Weldon Owen is a division of
BONNIER

Photographer Bill Bettencourt
Food Stylist Jen Straus
Photographer's Assistant Angelica Cao
Food Stylist's Assistant Alexa Hyman
Text Writer Stephanie Rosenbaum

ACKNOWLEDGMENTS
Weldon Owen wishes to thank the following people
for their generous support in producing this book:
Heather Belt, Kevin Crafts, Ken DellaPenta, Judith Dunham,
Denise Lincoln, Lesli Neilson and Sharon Silva.

ISBN-13: 978-1-61628-155-7 (paperback)
ISBN-10: 1-61628-155-3

ISBN-13: 978-1-61628-175-5 (hardcover)
ISBN-10: 1-61628-175-8

A NOTE ON WEIGHTS AND MEASURES
All recipes include customary U.S. and metric measurements. Metric conversions are based on
a standard developed for these books and have been rounded off. Actual weights may vary.